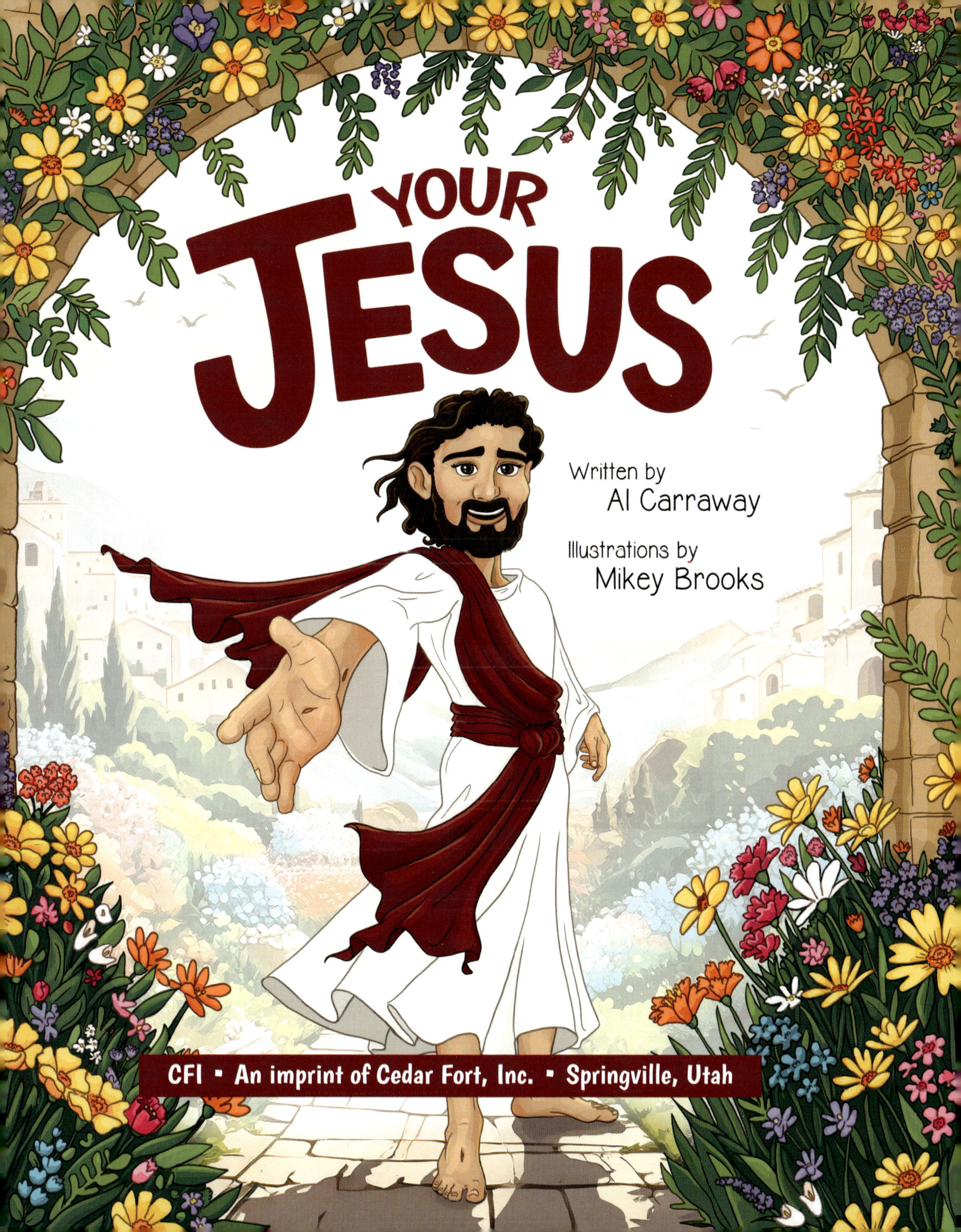
YOUR
JESUS
Written by
Al Carraway
Illustrations by
Mikey Brooks
CFI ▪ An imprint of Cedar Fort, Inc. ▪ Springville, Utah

I AM MARY.

I'm a girl from Nazareth—a small, quiet village. Who was I that God would choose me?

One day, a bright light appeared, and an angel stood before me. He said his name was Gabriel and that I shouldn't be afraid. God had chosen me to be the mother of Jesus, God's Son.

"Me? How could this be?" I wondered.

The angel told me that God was with me. The Holy Ghost would help me. And "with God, nothing is impossible."

I didn't understand it all, but I felt so blessed to be part of this miracle. God had "great things" in store for me.

Soon I would marry Joseph, a carpenter. He was a good man who loved me. The angel would visit Joseph in a dream and tell him to name the baby Jesus, meaning Savior because He would save the world!

GOD USES ORDINARY PEOPLE IN EXTRAORDINARY WAYS.

He may ask you to do difficult or unexpected things, but you are never alone. God is always with you.

When you act in trust and faith, He will help you do great things.

FEAR NOT.

With God, nothing is impossible.

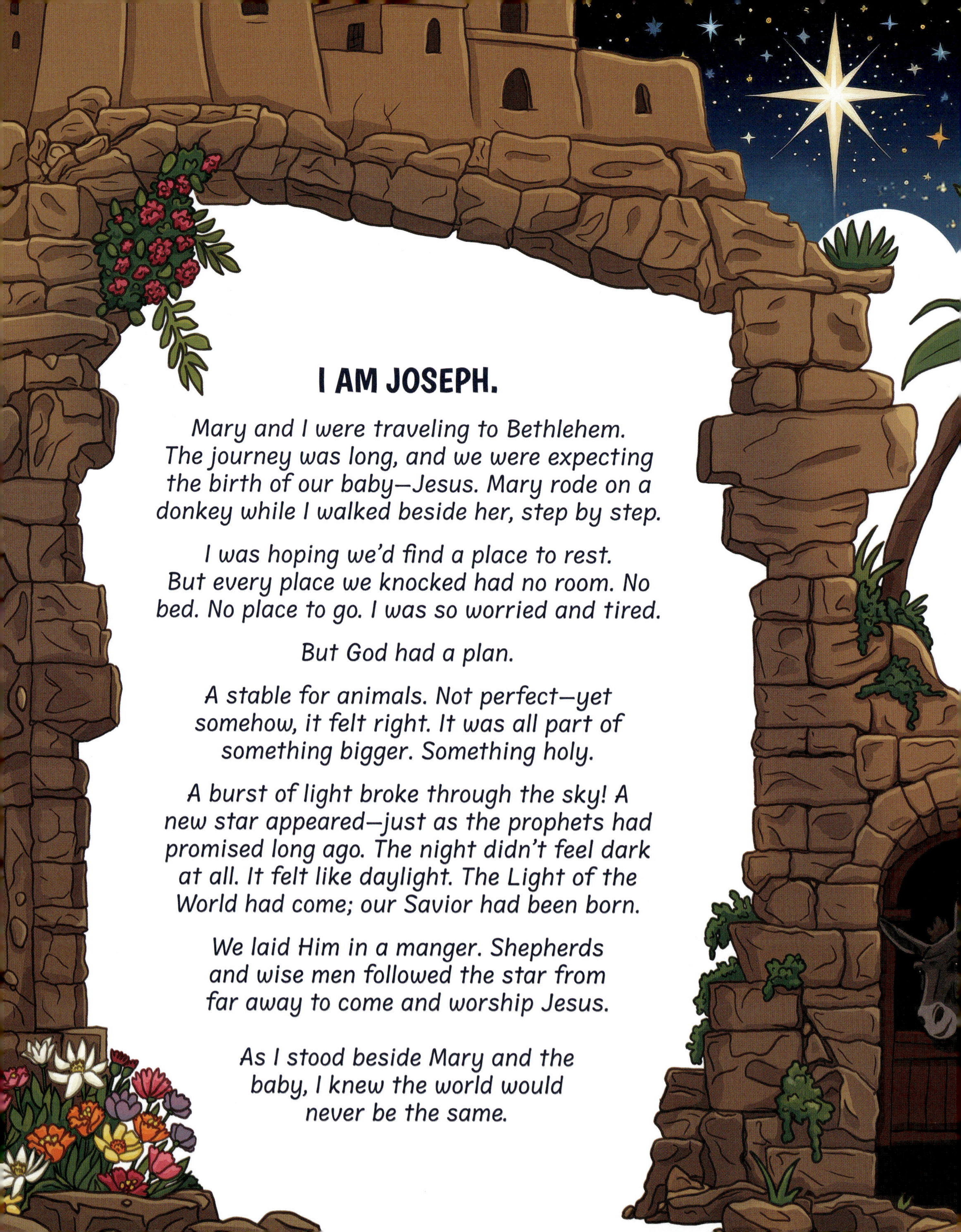

I AM JOSEPH.

Mary and I were traveling to Bethlehem. The journey was long, and we were expecting the birth of our baby—Jesus. Mary rode on a donkey while I walked beside her, step by step.

I was hoping we'd find a place to rest. But every place we knocked had no room. No bed. No place to go. I was so worried and tired.

But God had a plan.

A stable for animals. Not perfect—yet somehow, it felt right. It was all part of something bigger. Something holy.

A burst of light broke through the sky! A new star appeared—just as the prophets had promised long ago. The night didn't feel dark at all. It felt like daylight. The Light of the World had come; our Savior had been born.

We laid Him in a manger. Shepherds and wise men followed the star from far away to come and worship Jesus.

As I stood beside Mary and the baby, I knew the world would never be the same.

GOD IS ALWAYS MINDFUL OF YOU AND WHAT YOU ARE GOING THROUGH.
He is always taking care of you.

You can keep going, knowing there is something else to come. He fulfills all the words that His prophets have spoken.

And as you spend time turning to your Jesus, you will have light that guides you and drives out the dark.

YOU WILL BE BLESSED.

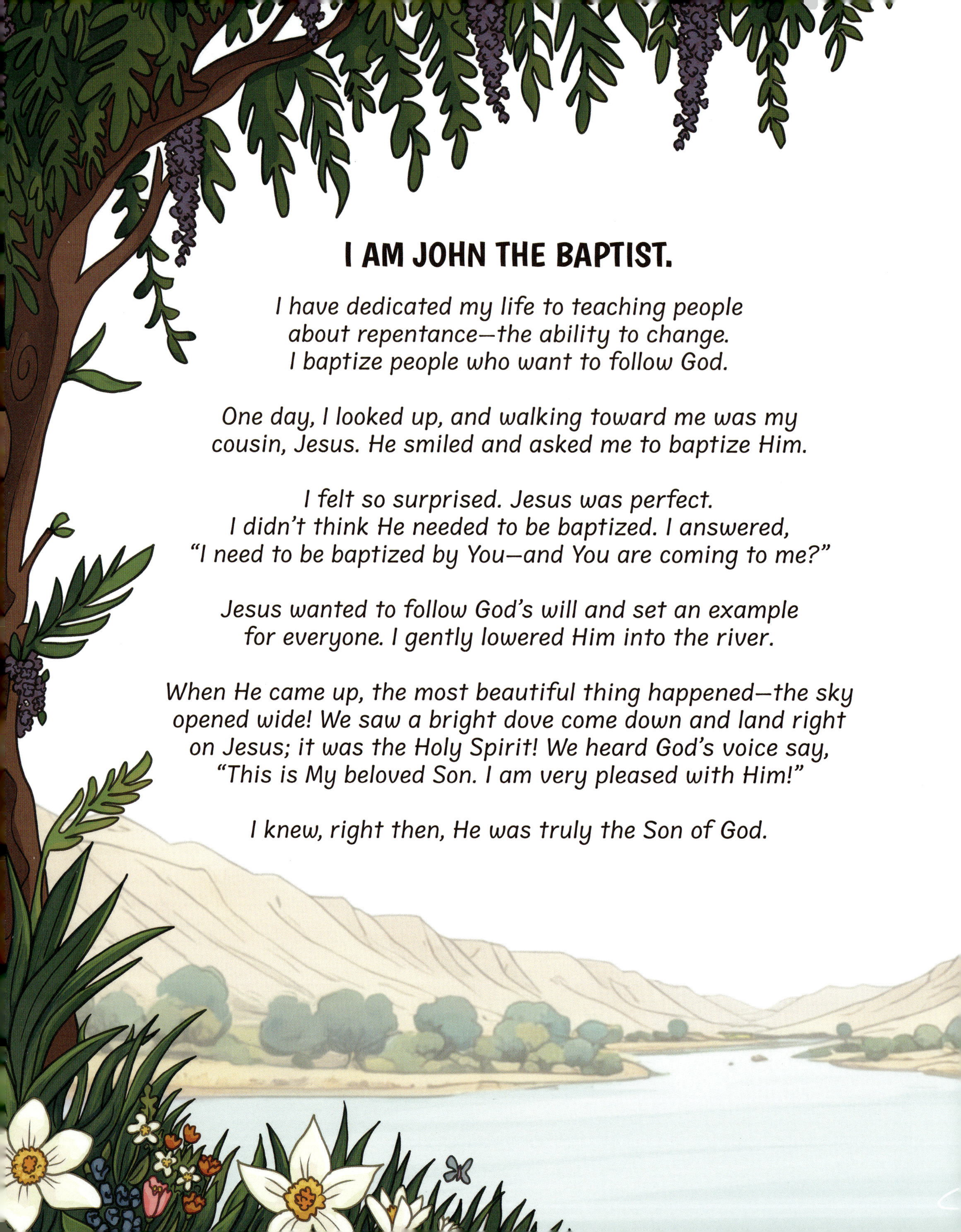

I AM JOHN THE BAPTIST.

I have dedicated my life to teaching people about repentance—the ability to change. I baptize people who want to follow God.

One day, I looked up, and walking toward me was my cousin, Jesus. He smiled and asked me to baptize Him.

I felt so surprised. Jesus was perfect. I didn't think He needed to be baptized. I answered, "I need to be baptized by You—and You are coming to me?"

Jesus wanted to follow God's will and set an example for everyone. I gently lowered Him into the river.

When He came up, the most beautiful thing happened—the sky opened wide! We saw a bright dove come down and land right on Jesus; it was the Holy Spirit! We heard God's voice say, "This is My beloved Son. I am very pleased with Him!"

I knew, right then, He was truly the Son of God.

YOUR JESUS COMES TO YOU.

And because of baptism, you can be forgiven.
You can always change for the better.

The Holy Ghost comes to you, too,
with guidance and comfort.

God is always mindful of you and is happy
when you follow the example of Jesus.

I AM PETER, A FISHERMAN.

I have several boats and men who work with me.

One night, no matter how hard we tried, we didn't catch a single fish. Not even one! I was so tired and discouraged. I was cleaning my nets, ready to give up for the night.

But then Jesus came! "Let down your nets," He called out.

Honestly, I didn't feel like trying again. But I decided to trust Him, so I let down my nets one more time.

And guess what? Suddenly, there were so many fish that the nets started to break. Our boats almost sank!

That's when Jesus told me He had bigger plans. He said, "From now on, you will be a fisher of men." He meant I would gather people and bring them closer to God.

Right then, I left my nets, my boats, everything—and I followed Jesus and became His discipple.

He promised I would see even greater things. And I believed Him.

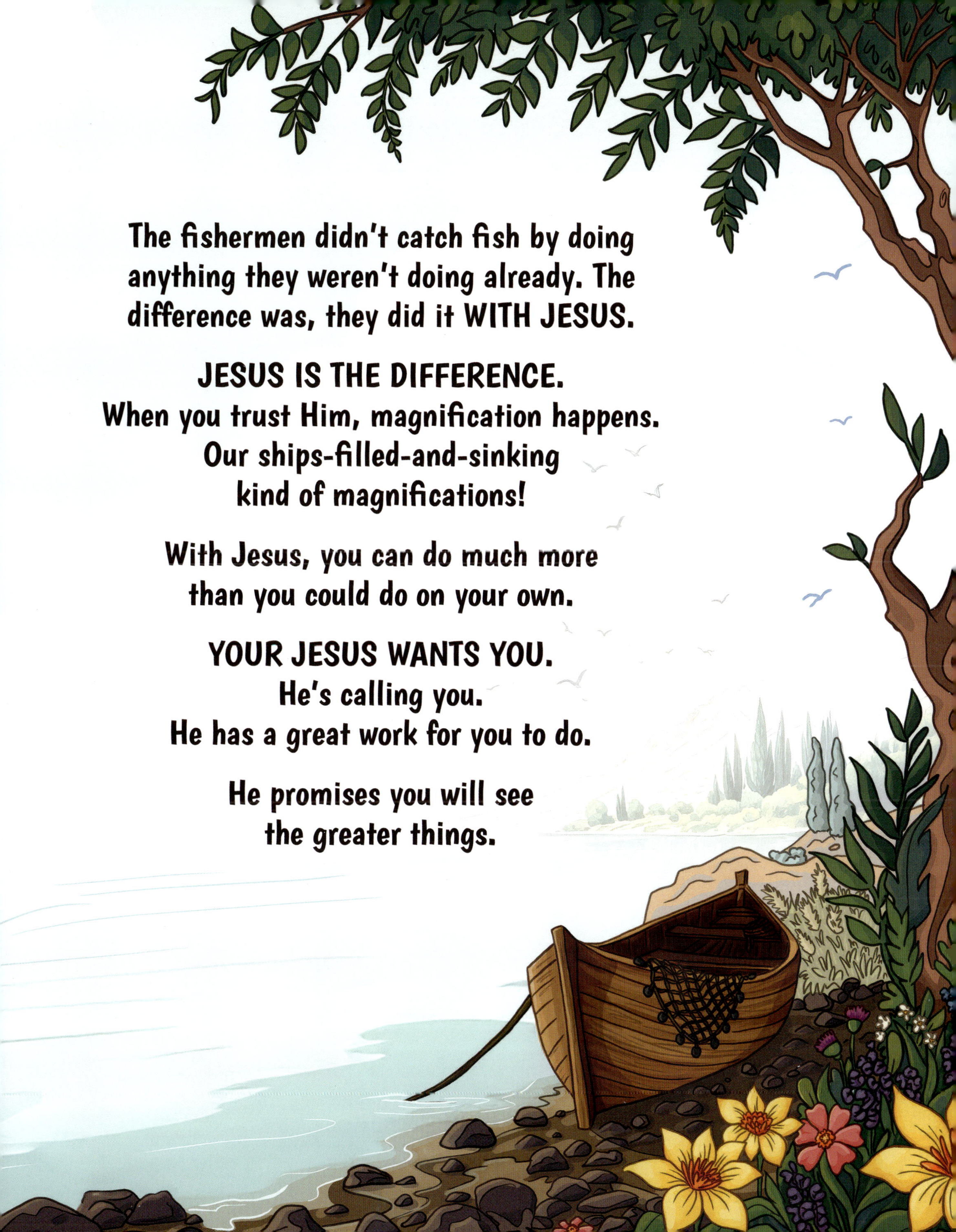

The fishermen didn't catch fish by doing anything they weren't doing already. The difference was, they did it **WITH JESUS.**

JESUS IS THE DIFFERENCE.
When you trust Him, magnification happens.
Our ships-filled-and-sinking
kind of magnifications!

With Jesus, you can do much more
than you could do on your own.

YOUR JESUS WANTS YOU.
He's calling you.
He has a great work for you to do.

He promises you will see
the greater things.

I AM MARY, AND I HAVE ANOTHER STORY TO TELL.

I was at a wedding with Jesus and lots of friends.

It was a happy day full of dancing, laughter, and celebration.

But then I noticed something; the food and drinks had run out, and the feast wasn't over yet. This was not good.

I immediately went to Jesus. I didn't know what He was going to do. I just knew He could help.

I turned to the servants and said gently, "Do whatever He tells you."

Jesus asked them to fill six large stone jars with water. These jars were usually used for people to wash and become spiritually clean.

The servants did as He said. And that's when Jesus changed the water into wine. And not just any wine—the very best wine anyone had ever tasted.

We all stood amazed, knowing we had witnessed Jesus's first miracle. I knew in my heart this was just the beginning!

Like Mary, when you turn to your Jesus,
He will be there to help with
what we cannot do on our own.

Because of Jesus, you can be cleansed,
you can change, and you can become better.

If you ever feel empty or lacking,
He will come to you and fill you.

He can replace the old and
transform it into new.

**BETTER THINGS ARE POSSIBLE
AND THEY ARE COMING.**

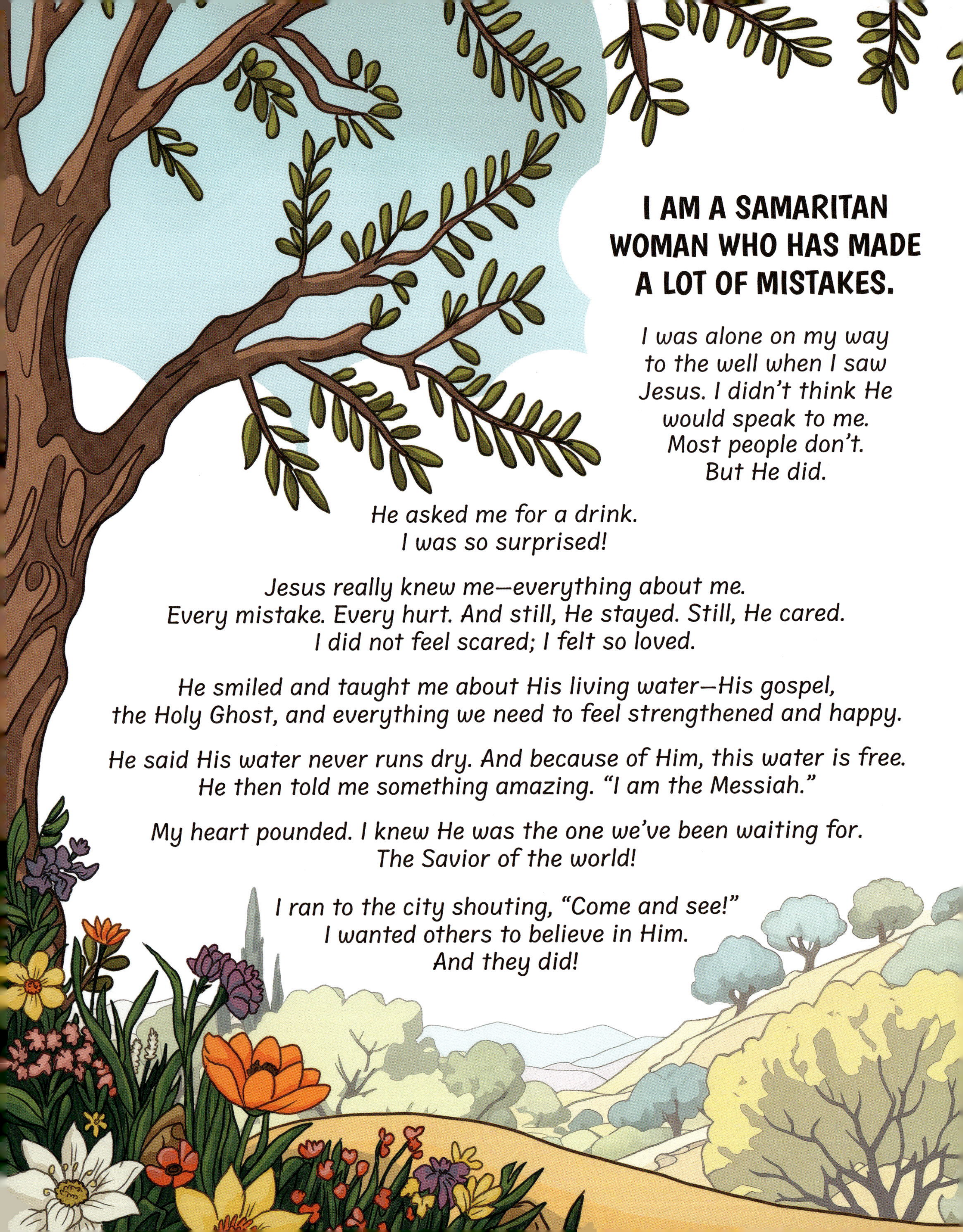

I AM A SAMARITAN WOMAN WHO HAS MADE A LOT OF MISTAKES.

I was alone on my way to the well when I saw Jesus. I didn't think He would speak to me. Most people don't. But He did.

He asked me for a drink. I was so surprised!

Jesus really knew me—everything about me. Every mistake. Every hurt. And still, He stayed. Still, He cared. I did not feel scared; I felt so loved.

He smiled and taught me about His living water—His gospel, the Holy Ghost, and everything we need to feel strengthened and happy.

He said His water never runs dry. And because of Him, this water is free. He then told me something amazing. "I am the Messiah."

My heart pounded. I knew He was the one we've been waiting for. The Savior of the world!

I ran to the city shouting, "Come and see!" I wanted others to believe in Him. And they did!

If you feel alone, your Jesus comes and spends time with you—even when you make mistakes.

Just as He offered Himself to her,
He offers Himself to you.

Just as Jesus taught of forgiveness,
your Jesus will cleanse and forgive you.

Just as He used her as a tool for His work,
He is in need of you as well.

WE CAN BE ANYTHING AND STILL BE WORTH IT TO HIM.

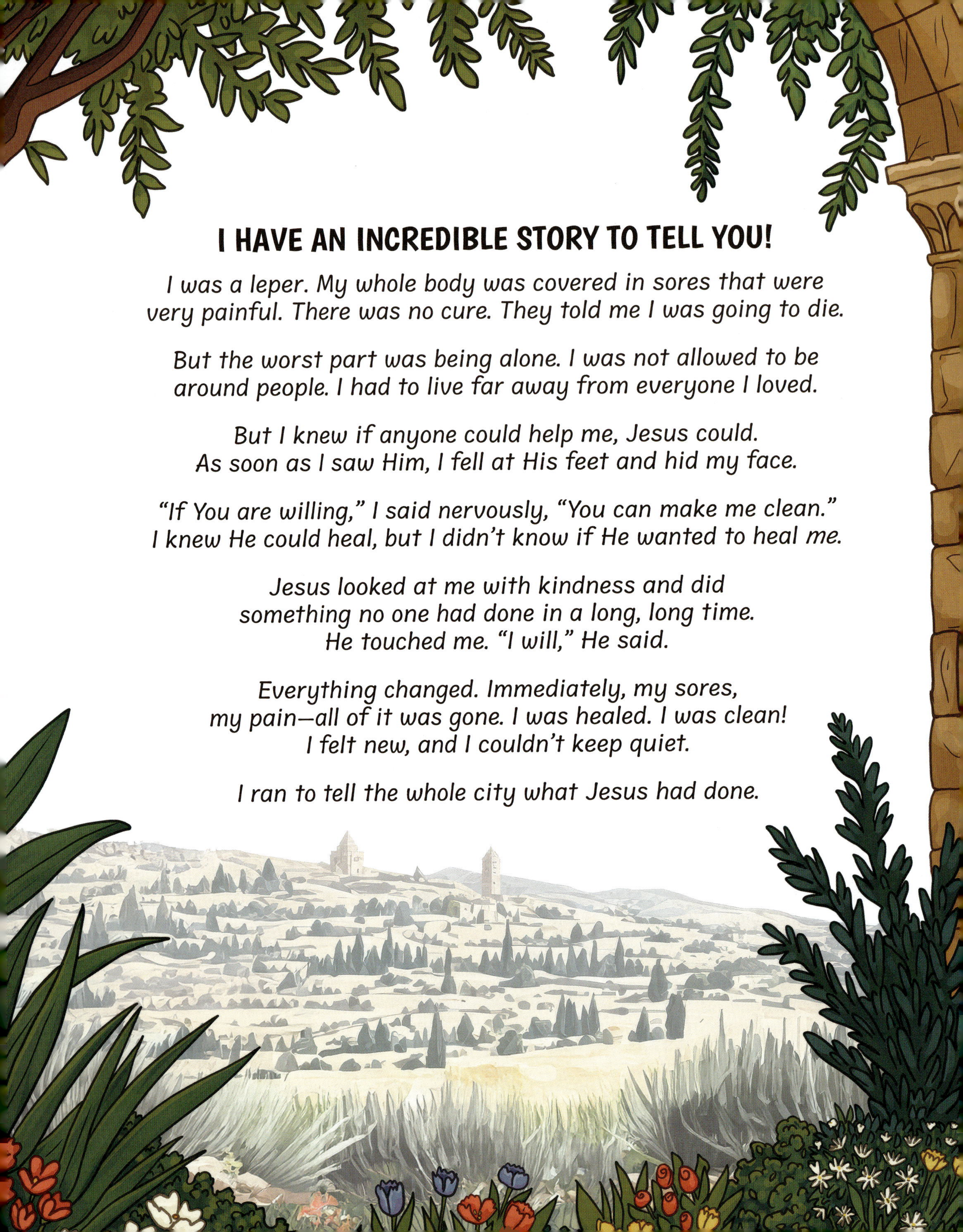

I HAVE AN INCREDIBLE STORY TO TELL YOU!

I was a leper. My whole body was covered in sores that were very painful. There was no cure. They told me I was going to die.

But the worst part was being alone. I was not allowed to be around people. I had to live far away from everyone I loved.

But I knew if anyone could help me, Jesus could. As soon as I saw Him, I fell at His feet and hid my face.

"If You are willing," I said nervously, "You can make me clean." I knew He could heal, but I didn't know if He wanted to heal me.

Jesus looked at me with kindness and did something no one had done in a long, long time. He touched me. "I will," He said.

Everything changed. Immediately, my sores, my pain—all of it was gone. I was healed. I was clean! I felt new, and I couldn't keep quiet.

I ran to tell the whole city what Jesus had done.

What may seem impossible to you
is not a struggle for your Jesus.

You may feel loneliness or pain, but when you go to Him,
He will ease that pain with love and compassion.

Things can improve. YOU can improve.

When everything and everyone says no,
JESUS SAYS, "I WILL."

Jesus touched the untouchable and cured the incurable.
Your struggles are never too much for Him.

I WAS A WOMAN WHO HAD BEEN SICK FOR TWELVE YEARS.

I was always bleeding.
I had seen so many doctors, but nothing helped.
I only got worse. I felt so discouraged and alone.
Maybe I would never be well again, I worried.

One day, a huge crowd filled the street, and that's when I saw Jesus. He was surrounded by many people, making His way through the streets.

Deep in my heart, I believed if I could just touch His clothes, I would be healed. So I reached. I stretched my hand through the crowd to touch even just the edge of His robe.

When I did, I felt a change inside me. Could it be? All these years of pain and sickness had disappeared in an instant. I was healed!

I didn't think He would notice me, hidden in the crowd. I felt so small—just one of many.

But Jesus, He stopped for me. He looked into my eyes and compassionately called me "daughter."

"Be of good comfort," He said.
"Your faith has made you whole. Go in peace."

And from that moment on, I was new.

Your Jesus knows you and what you are going through.
You are not hidden from Him.

HE NOTICES YOU.
He makes time for you.
He gives of Himself to you. Because you are His.

Your efforts and faith have real power.

His peace is meant for you, too.

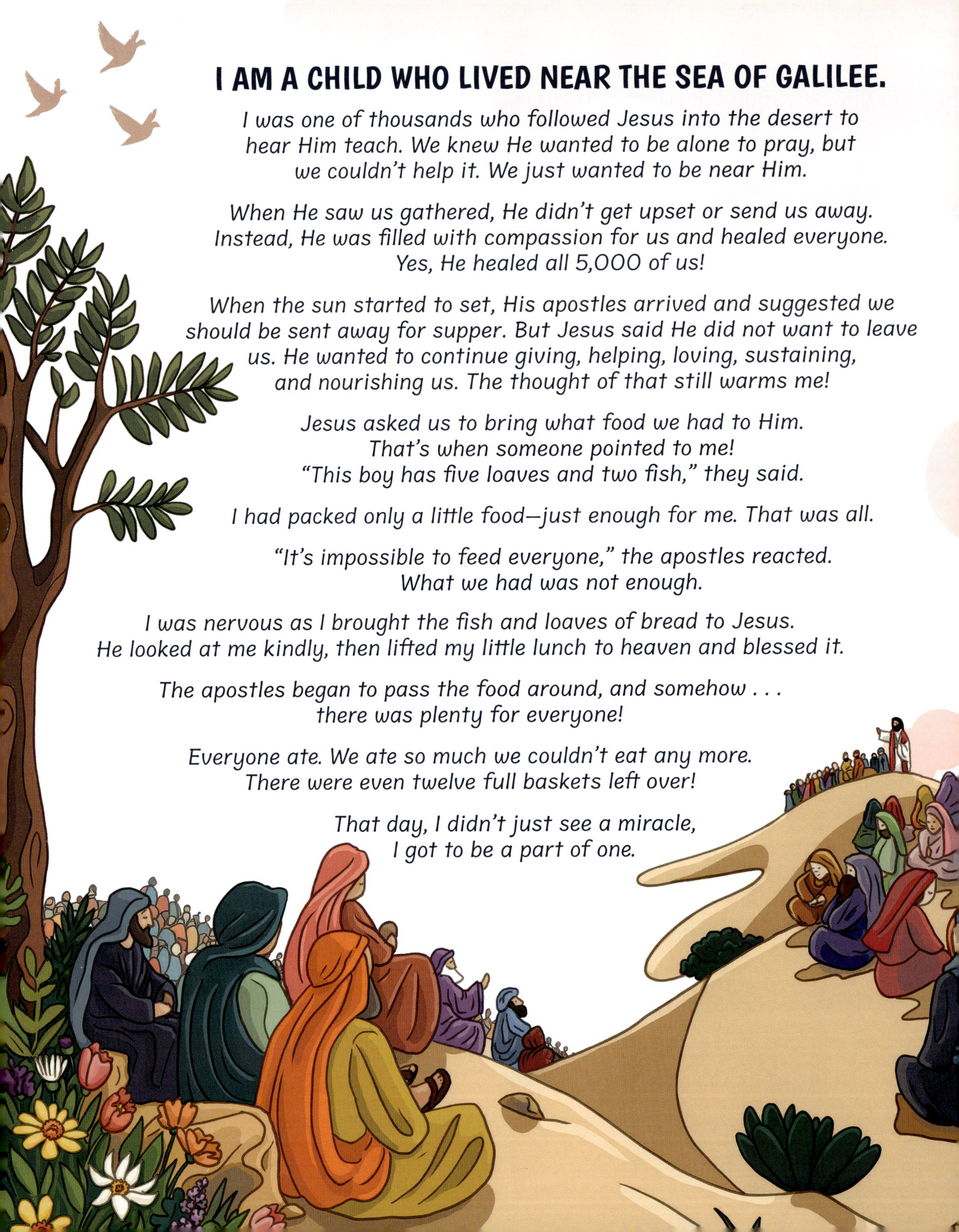

I AM A CHILD WHO LIVED NEAR THE SEA OF GALILEE.

I was one of thousands who followed Jesus into the desert to hear Him teach. We knew He wanted to be alone to pray, but we couldn't help it. We just wanted to be near Him.

When He saw us gathered, He didn't get upset or send us away. Instead, He was filled with compassion for us and healed everyone. Yes, He healed all 5,000 of us!

When the sun started to set, His apostles arrived and suggested we should be sent away for supper. But Jesus said He did not want to leave us. He wanted to continue giving, helping, loving, sustaining, and nourishing us. The thought of that still warms me!

Jesus asked us to bring what food we had to Him. That's when someone pointed to me! "This boy has five loaves and two fish," they said.

I had packed only a little food—just enough for me. That was all.

"It's impossible to feed everyone," the apostles reacted. What we had was not enough.

I was nervous as I brought the fish and loaves of bread to Jesus. He looked at me kindly, then lifted my little lunch to heaven and blessed it.

The apostles began to pass the food around, and somehow . . . there was plenty for everyone!

Everyone ate. We ate so much we couldn't eat any more. There were even twelve full baskets left over!

That day, I didn't just see a miracle, I got to be a part of one.

Your Jesus is filled with
compassion toward you.

He will not send you away.
He loves spending time with you.

When you are lacking, He provides healing
and nourishment until you are filled.

**WHATEVER YOU HAVE
TO OFFER IS ENOUGH.**

And your Jesus will give
back even more, still.

I AM PETER,
AND I HAVE ANOTHER STORY FOR YOU.

All twelve of us disciples were sailing the Sea of Galilee.

A very scary storm came.
The lightning lit up the entire sky. Wild waves towered high above us.

Our ship was tossed around most of the night.
It wasn't just that we were afraid of sinking, we were sinking.
I saw something in the distance, but I couldn't see through the rain.
I cried out in fear!

Then a voice called through the storm:
"Be of good cheer; it is Me, don't be afraid."

It was Jesus!
He was walking on the water, unaffected by the storm.
As soon as I knew it was my Savior, I wanted to go to Him.

"Come," He invited.

With my eyes fixed on Jesus,
I lifted my foot out of the boat and stepped onto the water.
I walked. Nothing else mattered except getting closer to Him.

But when I turned my gaze back to the waves,
the rain, and the storm, I was afraid again. I began to sink.

"Help me!" I cried.
Immediately, Jesus reached out His hand and saved me.
"Why would you doubt Me?" He asked.

But He wasn't angry that I sank.
He was passionately reminding me to always have faith in Him.

"I will always save you. You don't need to doubt that."

Then Jesus stopped the storm.
I know safety and saving come from reaching for Him.

Your Jesus stands untouched by the storms of
life with His focus set on you.

HE WANTS YOU TO GO TO HIM AT ALL TIMES.

Safety and peace come when you reach for His hand.
Your storms will be calmed.
You can do things that seem impossible.

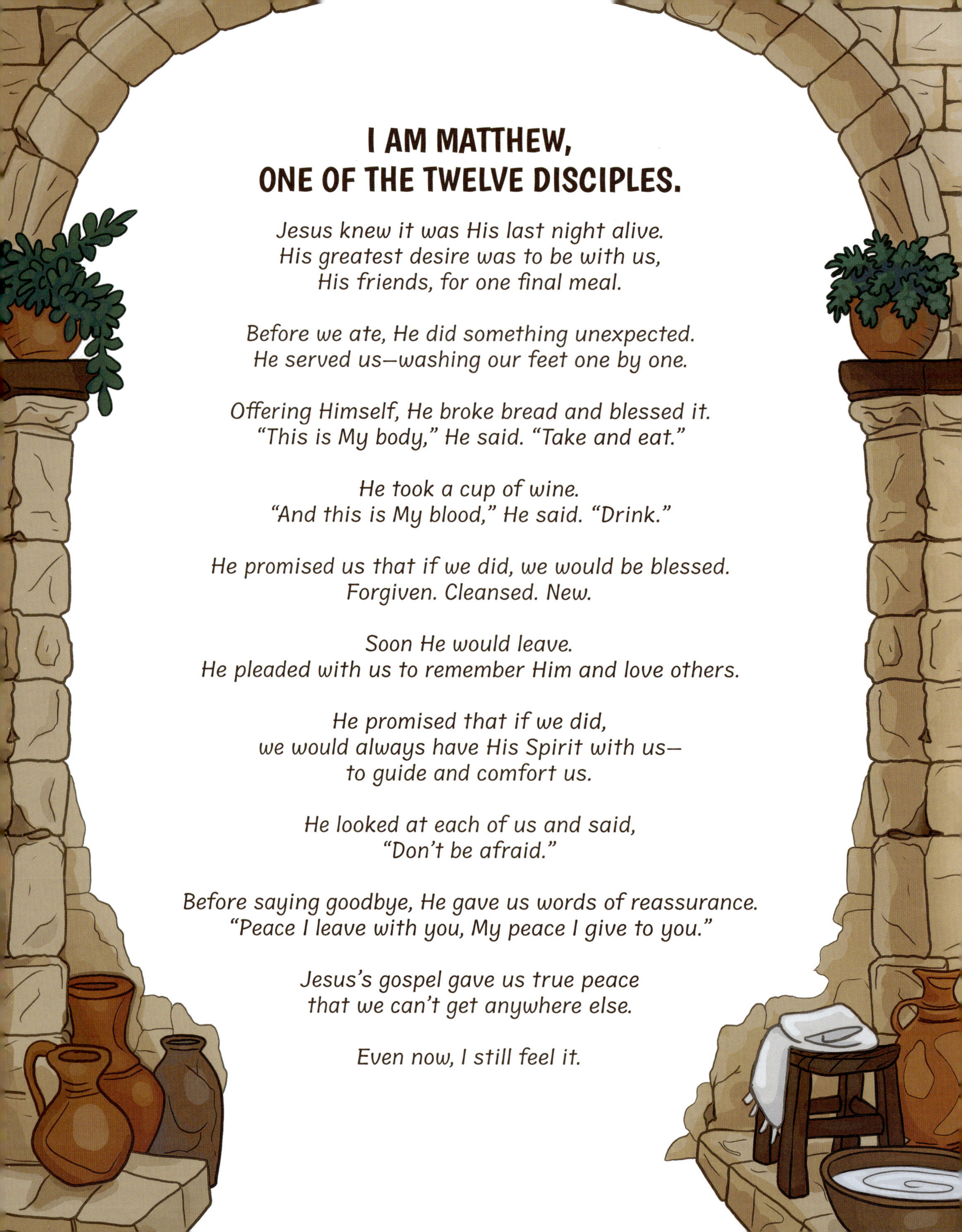

I AM MATTHEW,
ONE OF THE TWELVE DISCIPLES.

Jesus knew it was His last night alive.
His greatest desire was to be with us,
His friends, for one final meal.

Before we ate, He did something unexpected.
He served us—washing our feet one by one.

Offering Himself, He broke bread and blessed it.
"This is My body," He said. "Take and eat."

He took a cup of wine.
"And this is My blood," He said. "Drink."

He promised us that if we did, we would be blessed.
Forgiven. Cleansed. New.

Soon He would leave.
He pleaded with us to remember Him and love others.

He promised that if we did,
we would always have His Spirit with us—
to guide and comfort us.

He looked at each of us and said,
"Don't be afraid."

Before saying goodbye, He gave us words of reassurance.
"Peace I leave with you, My peace I give to you."

Jesus's gospel gave us true peace
that we can't get anywhere else.

Even now, I still feel it.

With love, your Jesus serves you.
Your Jesus offers Himself to you.
You can become one with Him.

When you remember Him,
you are blessed.

You can be forgiven and clean.
And with the Holy Ghost, His comfort and guidance will always be there for you.

You do not need to be afraid.
HE HAS PEACE TO GIVE YOU.

I AM JOHN THE BELOVED.

After our meal together, Jesus invited me, along with Peter and James, to go with Him into Gethsemane. That night in the garden, everything felt heavy. I had never seen Jesus like this before.

"My soul is sorrowful—even unto death. Stay here and watch," He said to us.

Jesus went a little farther and fell to the ground. We saw Him shake in pain. We heard Him cry out to His Father. We tried to stay awake to watch Him, but our eyes kept closing.

We were awakened when Jesus returned after being alone. His face was wet—not with sweat, but with blood. He had been suffering.

He had taken upon Himself our sins. Pain. Sickness. Loss. Temptations. All our troubles and worries. For me. For you. For everyone.

Jesus didn't run or shy away. He always knew His purpose was to save all mankind. He never lost sight of that. He never lost sight of us. And His suffering made that saving possible.

Three times He came back and found us sleeping. I may not have seen the angel that came, but that night in the garden, I saw what real love looks like.

You'll have times of pain and hurt.
There is nothing Jesus has not felt.
He has a perfect understanding of everything
you will feel and experience.

Your Jesus gave all that He had to give.
He held nothing back.

He gave all, so you can receive all.
To Him, it was worth it.

**TO JESUS, YOU
ARE WORTH IT.**

I WAS A THIEF.

I had done wrong. My punishment was a cross.

There were two others beside me, but one was different. His sign read: KING OF THE JEWS.

Crowds gathered, shouting cruel things at Him. Even the other thief joined in. I shouted back, "This man has done nothing wrong!"

But Jesus, even in His pain and unfair treatment, did not yell. He did not get angry. Instead, He shouted up to heaven, "Father, forgive them!"

Who is this man who pleads for forgiveness for those hurting Him?

In that moment, I believed the stories I had heard. I believed Jesus really was my Savior. And I hoped. *Could that forgiveness be for me, too?*

With humility, I dared to ask, "Jesus, Lord, remember me when You get to Your kingdom."

He looked at me with pure love. "Today, you will be with Me in paradise."

Peace and relief washed over me. I felt free.

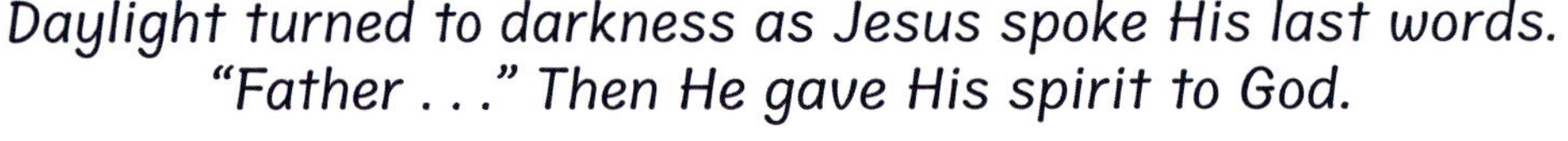

Daylight turned to darkness as Jesus spoke His last words. "Father . . ." Then He gave His spirit to God.

Even a Roman soldier testified, "Truly this was the Son of God."

Jesus died—but in dying, He brought us eternal life.

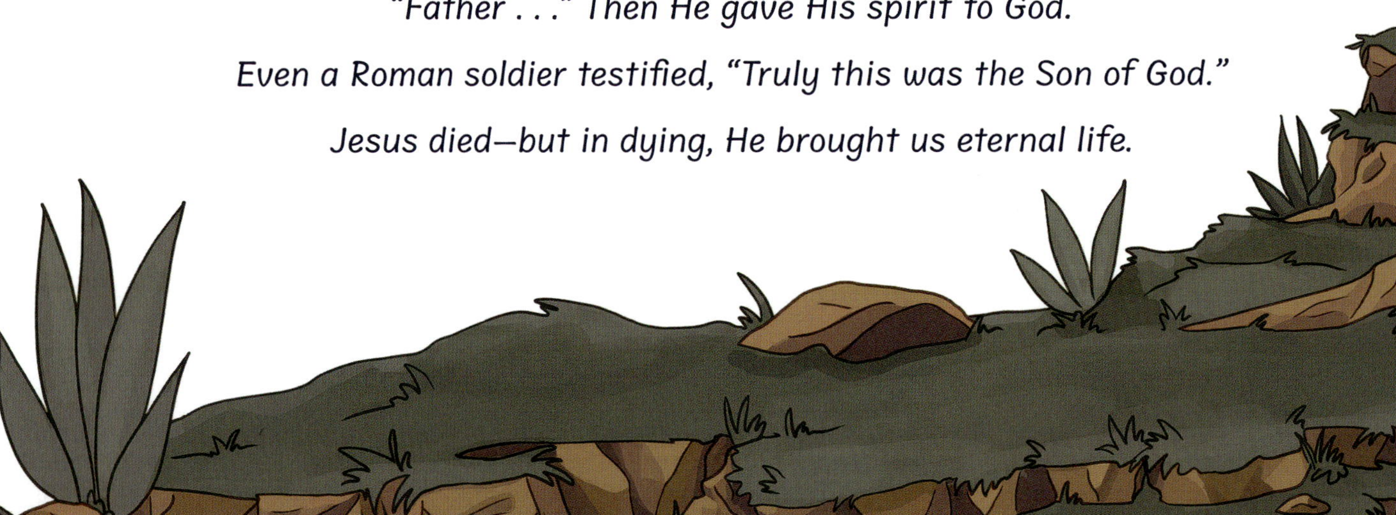

Because He chose the cross,
your Jesus also chose you.
He will always choose you.

With your hurt,
His peace is there for you.

With your mistakes,
His forgiveness is there for you.

His love will heal you.
HIS LOVE DOES HEAL YOU.

Your Jesus offers you His kingdom.
ALL IS NEVER LOST.

Still today, He gives of Himself.

We can feel free.

THE SKY WAS STILL DARK WHEN I LEFT.

But I couldn't wait any longer.
My heart was so heavy. I only wanted to
be near Jesus—near where His body lay.

But something didn't seem right. No guards. No stone.

I ran as fast as I could. Out of breath, with hands trembling,
I looked inside the tomb. Empty. Only the folded linens
remained. He was gone. Where is He? I wondered.
Has someone taken Him?
My heart broke all over again. I wept. I couldn't stop.

Two angels appeared. "Why are you crying?" they asked.
I could barely answer. "Tell me where they've taken Him."
"He is not here. He is risen," they said.

I turned and saw someone in the garden.
I couldn't recognize Him with the bright morning sun.

Then He said my name. "Mary."
In that one word, I knew. I gasped, "Master!"

It was Him. Jesus. My Lord. He had saved me before,
when my life was full of fear and darkness.
And now He had saved me again—everlastingly.

He was alive. Death did not win.

Later, He would appear to many.
He would show the wounds in His hands and His side.

But before all of that, He came to me.

In the quiet garden,
in the soft light of morning,
He called my name.

DEATH IS NOT THE END.
So much more is to come. It is beautiful.

He is still here.
He comes to you alive, active,
and promising to never leave.

And as you come closer to Him, He will
speak from His living lips—your name.

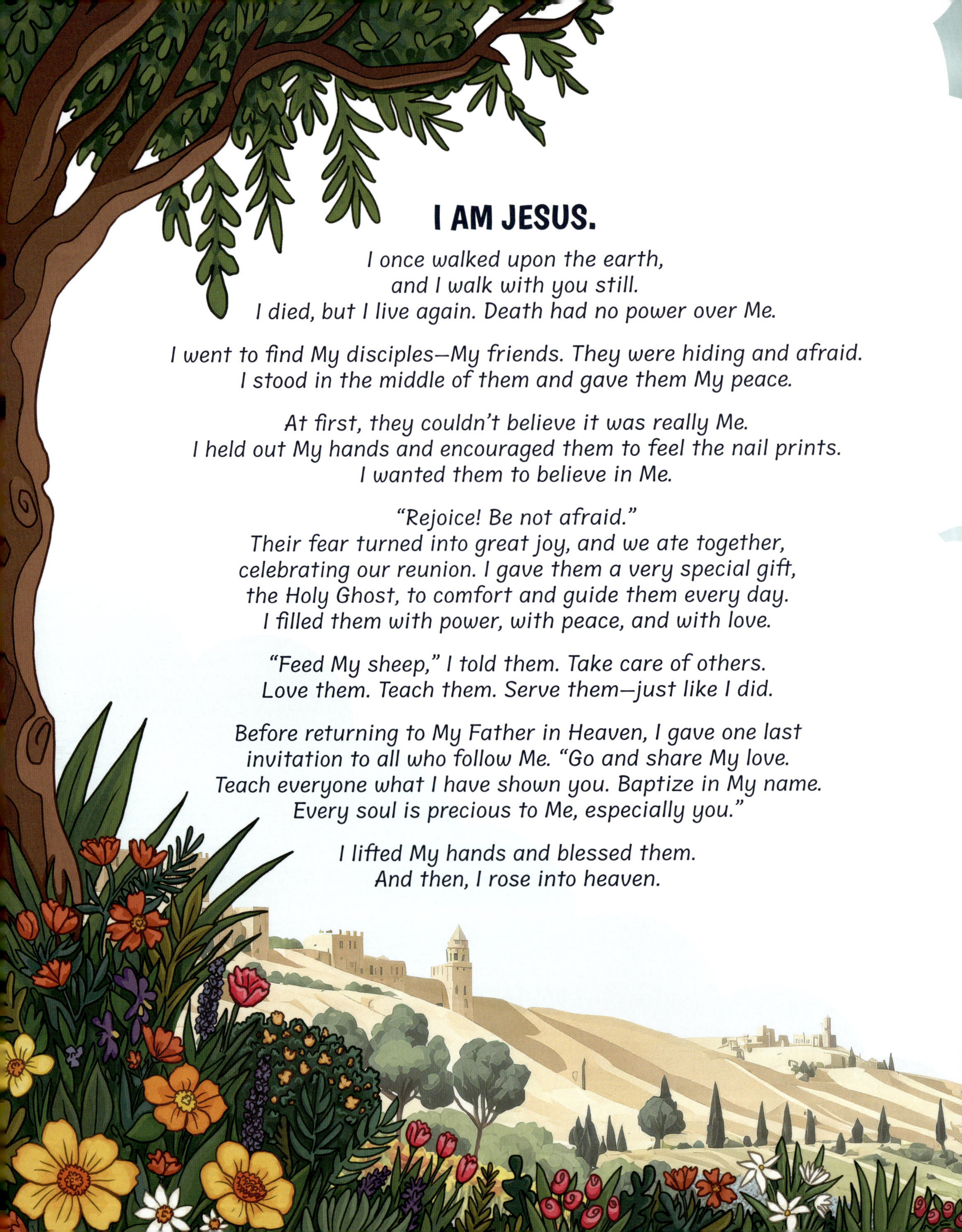

I AM JESUS.

I once walked upon the earth,
and I walk with you still.
I died, but I live again. Death had no power over Me.

I went to find My disciples—My friends. They were hiding and afraid.
I stood in the middle of them and gave them My peace.

At first, they couldn't believe it was really Me.
I held out My hands and encouraged them to feel the nail prints.
I wanted them to believe in Me.

"Rejoice! Be not afraid."
Their fear turned into great joy, and we ate together,
celebrating our reunion. I gave them a very special gift,
the Holy Ghost, to comfort and guide them every day.
I filled them with power, with peace, and with love.

"Feed My sheep," I told them. Take care of others.
Love them. Teach them. Serve them—just like I did.

Before returning to My Father in Heaven, I gave one last
invitation to all who follow Me. "Go and share My love.
Teach everyone what I have shown you. Baptize in My name.
Every soul is precious to Me, especially you."

I lifted My hands and blessed them.
And then, I rose into heaven.

But this is not the end.

You are Mine. I know you. I love you.
Believe in Me.

I am always with you.
I am your Jesus.

About the author

AL CARRAWAY is a multi-award-winning and #1 best-selling author of more than nine published titles, including Finding Yourself in the New Testament, Wildly Optimistic, and My Dear Little One—a Readers' Favorite International Gold Medal Winner.

Since 2011, Al has been an internationally acclaimed speaker, sharing her message in over 11 countries. She has a deep love for guiding Church history tours and speaking at faith-based seminars at sea.

Her passion is to tell everyone that happiness exists—and it comes from Jesus. He's real. He's tangible. And you can find and love Him in the hard, the unwanted, and the unexpected.

Originally from New York, she now lives in Pennsylvania with her husband and their three children. Learn more at alcarraway.com or follow her on Instagram: @alcarraway

About the illustrator

MIKEY BROOKS is an award-winning illustrator whose vibrant art can be found everywhere from wall murals to picture books. With a passion for children's art, he also explores various genres, creating magic on every page. When he's not illustrating or teaching art, he's busy writing—he's authored ten middle-grade novels and illustrated more than a dozen picture books.

Living in Utah with his wonderful wife, their six adorable kids, a plethora of fish, a three-legged dog, and a couple of invisible dragons, Mikey's life is a joyful adventure. Discover more about him and his whimsical creations at www.mikeybrooks.com.

ISBN 13: 978-1-4621-5042-7

Published by CFI, an imprint of Cedar Fort, Inc. • 2373 W. 700 S., Suite 100, Springville, UT 84663
Distributed by Cedar Fort, Inc., www.cedarfort.com

Cover design and interior layout by Shawnda T. Craig

Printed in the United States of America • Printed on acid-free paper

10 9 8 7 6 5 4 3 2 1